NO
SE

D0722760

Dealing with Feeling...
Caring

Isabel Thomas

Illustrated by Clare Elsom

Heinemann
LIBRARY
Chicago, Illinois

© 2013 Heinemann Library
an imprint of Capstone Global Library, LLC
Chicago, Illinois

To contact Capstone Global Library please
phone 800-747-4992, or visit our website
www.capstonepub.com

All rights reserved. No part of this publication may
be reproduced or transmitted in any form or by
any means, electronic or mechanical, including
photocopying, recording, taping, or any information
storage and retrieval system, without permission in
writing from the publisher.

Edited by Dan Nunn, Rebecca Rissman, and
 Catherine Veitch
Designed by Philippa Jenkins
Original illustrations © Clare Elsom
Illustrated by Clare Elsom
Production by Victoria Fitzgerald
Originated by Capstone Global Library, Ltd.
Printed in China

16 15 14 13 12
10 9 8 7 6 5 4 3 2 1

Library of Congress Cataloging-in-Publication Data
Thomas, Isabel, 1980-
 Caring / Isabel Thomas.
    p. cm.—(Dealing with feeling)
 Includes bibliographical references and index.
 ISBN 978-1-4329-7104-5 (hb)—ISBN 978-1-4329-7113-7 (pb) 1. Caring in children—Juvenile literature. 2. Caring—Juvenile literature. I. Title.
 BF723.C25T56 2013
 177'.7—dc23   2012008276

Every effort has been made to contact copyright
holders of material reproduced in this book. Any
omissions will be rectified in subsequent printings if
notice is given to the publisher.

All the Internet addresses (URLs) given in this book
were valid at the time of going to press. However,
due to the dynamic nature of the Internet, some
addresses may have changed, or sites may have
changed or ceased to exist since publication. While
the author and publisher regret any inconvenience
this may cause readers, no responsibility for any such
changes can be accepted by either the author or
the publisher.

Contents

Some words are shown in bold, **like this.** Find out what they mean in the glossary on page 23.

What Does Being Caring Mean?

Everybody has **feelings**. Being caring means that you care about other people's feelings.

Caring people like to help other people feel good. They are being caring when they help others.

What Does It Feel Like to Be Caring?

Caring people feel bad when someone else is sad, angry, worried, or lonely. They try to help people feel better.

Helping people feel good makes you feel good, too. Being caring also helps you make new friends.

How Can I Be Caring?

You can be caring every day. Look for ways to help other people.

Caring people know when things are fair or unfair. They do their best to make things fair.

How Do Rules Help Me to Be Caring?

A caring person knows that rules help to make things fair for everyone. You can be caring by **obeying** rules.

You can be caring by helping with **housework,** even when it is not your turn. Being caring means putting other people before yourself.

How Can I Help My Friends to Feel Happy?

What do you do when your friends are sad or worried? Caring people make time to listen to their friends.

Be a good listener by asking questions. Look at people when they speak and don't **interrupt.**

How Can I Help Other People to Feel Happy?

Imagine that a new child joins your class. The child might be sad, scared, or shy.

You can be caring by speaking to the new child. A caring person makes sure nobody feels left out.

What If I Get Mad at Someone?

It is okay to feel angry sometimes. Thinking about how the other person feels will make you feel better. Perhaps the person did not mean to upset you.

Caring people say sorry when they have been unkind to somebody. Being caring means being **forgiving**.

What Should I Do If Someone Is Not Being Caring?

Being caring means doing the right thing. If you see someone being unkind, the right thing to do is to tell a grown-up.

You can help by being kind to children who have been **bullied.** A caring person does not tease or bully people.

How Can Being Caring Make Me Happy?

Caring people are good friends to have.
They are there when you need them.

If you are caring and helpful, people
will share things with you. Being a
good friend will help make you feel
happy, too!

Make a Caring Toolbox

Write down some tips to help you care for others.

Notice when someone else is sad, mad, worried, or lonely.

Be a good listener.

Put other people before yourself.

Tell a grown-up if you see someone being unkind.

Include other people in your games.

Be friendly to children you don't know.

Look for ways to help people.

Share and wait your turn.

Glossary

bullied to be harmed or made fun of by somebody

feeling something that happens inside our minds. It can affect our bodies and the way we behave.

forgiving stop being angry with someone who has upset you

housework jobs that need to be done around your home

imagine make a picture in your head

interrupt stop somebody who is speaking by starting to speak yourself

obeying doing what a rule or grown-up says you are supposed to do

Find Out More

Books

Raatma, Lucia. *Caring* (21st Century Junior Library). Ann Arbor, Mich.: Cherry Lake, 2009.

Stead, Philip. *A Sick Day for Amos McGee.* New York: Roaring Brook, 2010.

Internet sites

Facthound offers a safe, fun way to find Internet sites related to this book. All of the sites on Facthound have been researched by our staff.

Here's all you do:
Visit www.facthound.com
Type in this code: 9781432971045

Index